THE
Archive Photographs
SERIES

BISHOP
AUCKLAND

The gateway to the Bishop's Park, c.1950, built by Bishop Trevor in the eighteenth century.

THE
Archive Photographs
SERIES

BISHOP
AUCKLAND

Compiled by
John Land

CHALFORD

The Chalford Publishing Company
St Mary's Mill, Chalford,
Stroud, Gloucestershire, GL6 8NX

ISBN 0 7524 0312 5

Typesetting and origination by
The Chalford Publishing Company
Printed in Great Britain by
Redwood Books, Trowbridge

Bishop Trevor's coat of arms. The sword and the coronet are significant, showing he was a Prince Bishop.

Contents

Acknowledgements

The author would like to thank the following individuals and organisations without whose help this book could never have been produced.

Gillian Wales and her staff at Durham County Library,
Bishop Auckland Town Hall;
Alastair Yule, the warden of Auckland Castle;
Dr. Bob McManners, Chairman of the Bishop Auckland Civic Society,
for permission to use pictures from the Frank Hutchinson Collection;
Sid Wigham for pictures from his own extensive collection
and Ted Teasdale for the pictures they contributed.

My sincere thanks also go to
Gavin Bake, Alan Barker, Marion Blackett, Richard Boothroyd,
Crook History Society, Courtauld Institute of Art,
Durham County Council Arts,
Museums and Libraries Department Staff at Darlington,
Eileen Elgey, Dorothy Goundray, Joan Hebdon,
Laurel and Hardy Museum Ulveston, Trevor Lee, Eddie and Adele Rossi,
John Sygrove, Phil Trussler, Wear Valley District Council, Fred Wilkinson,
Irene Wilkinson, and last but by no means least Ann Wood.

There will be names I have not mentioned, largely people who have donated pictures to the collection over the years. To them and to anyone else I may have missed out, I offer my apologies but also my thanks.

Introduction

Look at the history of Bishop Auckland and you will see the history of England in a nutshell. Roman soldiers marched along Dere Street, now Newgate Street the main shopping area, and Saxons built a church at Escomb near the River Wear. A twelfth century Bishop of Durham, Hugh de Puiset, built a hunting lodge so that Norman nobles could chase deer and wild boar and from that the town grew.

For centuries the North East of England was a battleground - the kingdom's northern border frequently raided by the Scots. The Bishops of Durham were created princes to hold a 'buffer state' for the monarch. They could raise their own armies, mint their own money and administer their own justice. These were the powerful men who influenced the growth of Auckland Castle and the town. Today people enjoy a walk in the beautiful Bishop's Park but on the night of 16 October 1346 the English army camped there before the Battle of Neville's Cross.

In Henry VIII's time Bishop Auckland was in a turmoil because of religion. Five men of the town and 39 others from the surrounding area were executed for taking part in the 'Pilgrimage of Grace', a northern uprising against the king's break from Rome and his new taxes. During the Commonwealth prominent Parliamentarian Sir Arthur Hazelrigg administered the north east while living at Auckland Castle and King Charles I stayed in the town on his way to London to be tried and beheaded.

While the church was the greatest influence on early Bishop Auckland, new commercial influences came with the Industrial Revolution. The birth of the railways, ironworks and coal mining turned Bishop Auckland into a boom town during the Victorian era. A new class of industrialist and businessman opened mines, banks and factories. The people who worked for them formed community groups and organised their sports. For a night out they went to the music hall, the theatre, the cinema and the bingo halls. Then they bought television and the places of entertainment closed down.

The book can only give a glimpse at Bishop Auckland's history but hopefully it will entertain and perhaps give some readers the desire to find out more.

One

A walk around
Bishop Auckland

Market Place, Bishop Auckland 1862.

An aerial view of Bishop Auckland, c.1970 from the north. The long straight line of Newgate Street and Cockton Hill Road was originally part of the Roman Dere Road.

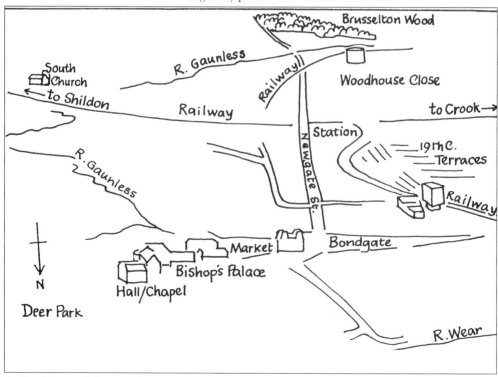

A sketch map of the aerial view.

The Market Place, formerly St. Anne's Green, c.1860 showing the town pant (water supply) and the stocks. The cottages left of the church were pulled down to build the Town Hall.

Backhouse's Bank, Market Place, 1870. J. Blackhouse, the Darlington banker, opened this branch in 1868. It amalgamated with Barclay's Bank in 1896.

The winning design for Bishop Auckland Town Hall in the early 1860s. London architect John Phillpot Jones collected a £20 prize but his design was modified by local architect John Johnstone for the actual building.

The Town Hall and Market Place, c.1900.

The fair comes to the town at the turn of the century.

The annual fair drew crowds to the Market Place from around the area. The steam traction engines driving the roundabouts also powered the fairground organs which were the centrepieces of these rides. Murphy's, in the background, visited the town for many generations.

A busy Bishop Auckland market day, c.1950. The Thursday and Saturday markets have always been popular, attracting shoppers from a wide area in south west Durham.

Gill's shop and the Castle Hotel in the Market Place, c.1960. Gill's, established in 1875, was one of the town's most prominent businesses. It's huge sign, on the gable end of the building, left, could be seen from the top of the long and straight Newgate Street, half a mile away.

A very old picture of the north east corner of the Market Place. The cobbled street is now tarmaced but Wear Chare, the road that runs between the two hostelriesdown to the river Wear, is still as steep as ever. The building on the right, then owned by Thomas Robson, is still recognisable today as the Sportsman Inn. The Eagle Tavern, owned by William Stevens on the left, is long gone but standing there today is Harvey's, one of the town's top nightspots. Do things really change ?

Doggart's department store, Market Place, c.1960. The huge Bishop Auckland store was the headquarters of the firm which had other branches throughout the country. The store, which carried a vast and varied stock, went through to Newgate Street where there were other entrances. 'Bishop Auckland has never been the same since Doggart's closed' is a comment still heard today.

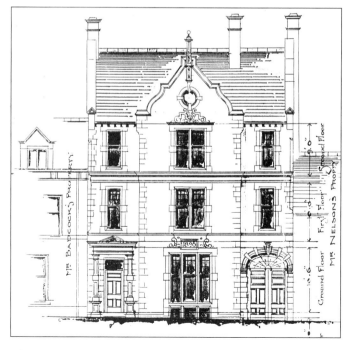

Plans for King's Lodge built in 1895 for local businessman Mr J. Thornborough in King Street behind the Town Hall. A sensitive conversion has recently turned the building into attractive flats.

The Elms, a Georgian house off the Market Place, pictured in the 1970s. Until recently it was used as offices by Wear Valley Distrct Council. The picture is taken from King Street, named after King Charles I who was held prisoner nearby.

Bus stands, with a popular snack bar, in the Market Place in 1983 before the opening of the bus station.

On the right are the old almshouses near the entrance to Auckland Castle, c.1950.

Victorian houses behind the Town Hall, c.1960. The plaque on the wall refers to Edward Maltby, Bishop of Durham from 1836 to 1856.

Wear Chare, c.1960. The steep, narrow Lane leads from the Market Place down to the river Wear, the Batts and Vinovium, the Roman fort.

The Batts in flood, January 1982. The Batts was originally used for archery pratice and later, by the local militia, for shooting practice. The worst flood was in 1771 when the hamlet of Jock's Row was washed away.

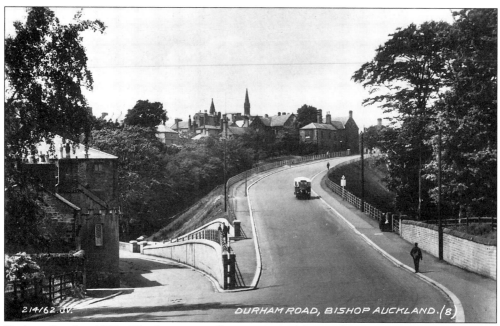

Durham Road, c.1930s. The bus is travelling on part of the road improved in the 1920s. The original road, on the left, was the route taken by packhorses carrying lead and coal from the area.

The demolition of Ferens Mill, c.1970. This old flour mill stood on the banks of the river Gaunless just off the Durham Road.

Brack's Wood, c.1910 - a favourite walk for local people.

Bishop Auckland's main police station and courts, c.1940. This site in Bondgate was later cleared and a new police station and courts built further out of the town centre.

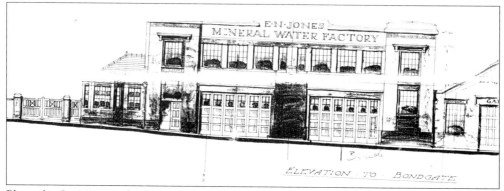

Plans for Jones' pop factory which stood in North Bondgate in 1939. The factory was demolished to make way for a car park.

A fine old Bishop Auckland building pictured in the 1960s. It looks Elizabethan but where was it and why didn't someone save it ?

The old summerhouse behind 4 to 6 High Bondgate seen in the 1970s. It is thought to be one of two former observatories in the town; the other, now demolished, being in Etherley Lane.

Part of Newton Cap, c.1960. Newton Cap was one of the earliest settlements which formed the township of Bishop Auckland.

Skirlaw Bridge, in the foreground, was built by Bishop Walter Skirlaw (1388-1406) to replace an older bridge. It spans the river Wear, joining Bishop Auckland to Toronto.

Dam Head, c.1960. The dam directed water from the river Wear into the water works at West Mills. To the left was a fish ladder, enabling salmon and sea trout to migrate up river. The pool below the dam was called '21 foot', a favourite swimming place.

24

Dam Head and Water Works, Bishop Auckland.

Dam Head and the water works, c.1930. Surrounded by trees and landscaped gardens, the Victorian water works were the pride of a town which had relied on springs and wells. The cholera epidemics of the 1830s and 1840s forced the Board of Health to improve the water supply.

A bus crossing Skirlaw Bridge, c.1930. The houses on the left are Newton Cap and on the right, Town Head. The chimney, left, is part of Newton Cap brickworks.

Skirlaw Bridge and the railway viaduct, 1860. The vaiduct, opened just after this picture was taken, carried trains until 1968 when the railway closed. In July 1995, with imaginative restoration, the viaduct was re-opened as a road bridge.

Old Newton Cap Hall, c.1860. The hall is believed to have dated back to the 1650s. Families associated with it include the Wrens, Bacons and Drummonds. The Industrial Revolution finally put pay to it when it was pulled down and the stone used to build coke ovens.

Newgate Street from the Market Place, c.1950, when many shops were privately owned and the street was open to traffic.

Newgate Street, c.1970. The upper storeys of the buildings show the street's wide variety of architectural styles.

McIntyre's shop in Newgate Street sold shoes and leather goods for over one hundred years. Seen here in the 1950s, it only recently closed down. The style of the façade has been kept by the new owners.

The Black Horse Hotel, c.1950. At one time there 57 pubs in the town - 20 in Newgate Street and a further 17 within a few yards of the main street.

Victoria Avenue, looking towards Newgate Street, c.1960. On the left is the former Temperance Hall, the Mechanics Institute, built in 1880, and the Co-operative Jubilee Hall with its wrought iron canopy.

Lingford's grocers shop, Newgate Street, c.1950. The Harrod's food hall of the town, it enticed shoppers inside with its aroma of freshly roasted coffee.

Newgate Street at the turn of the century showing houses as well as commercial premises.

Newgate Street in the early 1900s showing the rapid growth of trade.

Newgate Street, c.1905. Finlay's jewellers still trade today.

Newgate Street, c.1905. The absence of traffic allowed men to gossip in the roadway.

Staff of Fred Robinson's shoe shop, 1901. It is still a local business.

FRED ROBINSON'S
COLOSSAL SALE OF BOOTS & SHOES
AT
43, Newgate Street, Bishop Auckland.

The before mentioned articles are only a few of our SPECIAL LINES. Our shop is the largest in Bishop Auckland in the Boot trade, and we will be pleased to show anyone our stock (we don't charge anything for looking at it), we know you can't resist BUYING when once you've seen it.

Important Notice!

Owing to the extremely LOW PRICES we are asking for goods during this Sale, we cannot allow any articles to be Booked, or any Approval Parcels at Sale Prices; our stock must be sold and everything be cleared out. We ask all customers will take note of this. We will do our best to please you in the shop, and will exchange any goods which are returned in good condition within a week.

N.B.—I have also leased the shop lately occupied by Mr. Arridge, No. 39, Newgate Street (between the May-Pole Dairy Co. and my Repairing Shop), and will be pleased to see all my customers there when I open out.

Don't forget our Repairing Establishment!
Anybody's Boots made as good as new!
☞ Only Best English Leather used!

☞ Don't forget the date, July the 18th.
THE ONLY ADDRESS:
Fred Robinson,
THE OLD ESTABLISHED FIRM,
40, 41, 43, NEWGATE STREET,
BISHOP AUCKLAND.

FRED ROBINSON'S
GIGANTIC REMOVAL
SALE

THE PREMISES:
43, NEWGATE STREET,
BISHOP AUCKLAND.
Having been up for Sale, we must clear all our
TREMENDOUS STOCK
(Valued at nearly £3,000) before removing.

Every pair must either be sold or given away before
☞ 13th AUGUST, 1901.
THE SALE COMMENCES
Thursday, July 18th,
And see our Windows on that date for Bargains.

All Goods are reduced 20 per cent. below cost.

THE GOODS OFFERED AT THIS
COLOSSAL SALE
Are not shoddy stuff bought specially for it, but regular Stock lines at Prices which cannot be equalled in Bishop Auckland or any other town.

Fred Robinson's removal sale, starting Thursday 18th July 1901, sounded well worth going to.

The Bishop Auckland Industrial Co-operative Flour and Provision Society Ltd. Their central shop opened in 1883 with a tea party in the Town Hall for 3,000 people.

The Co-op's Newgate Street store was extended in 1894; an extension opened by the treasurer Mr. J. Parkin.

The Co-op tobacco factory in Durham Street opened in November 1898 under the management of Mr. James Tait. It employed six men and sixteen women.

The Co-op bakery, opened in 1910, was designed to produce 52,000 loaves per week.

St. Peter's Church, Princes Street, c.1960.
Built in 1875, in a rapidly developing area
of the town, it saw the baptism of Stan
Laurel of Laurel and Hardy fame.

The town's sole surviving air raid shelter, in East Parade, c.1960.

The construction of Vinovium House, Tenters Street, c.1970. It is still regarded as the town's biggest eyesore. On the right is the old Odeon cinema, later demolished to make way for a supermarket.

An 1857 Pollards cottage on Etherley Lane, c.1980. It stands on Pollards Lands - an area of the town given to John Pollard for killing a wild boar that rampaged through the Bishop's estates in medieval times.

The Edwardian bandstand in the town recreation ground, c.1979. It now graces a park in Gateshead.

Bell's chocolate shop in Newgate Street, c.1920. It was part of the former Lyric Picture Palace. Ethel Bell, the owner, worked seven days a week until 11p.m. when she caught the last bus home to West Auckland.

Peter Pell's new shop opened in Bishop Auckland in 1957 providing the customer with a good choice of raincoats.

Self service grocery stores came to Bishop Auckland in 1959.

Rossi's cafe and ice-cream parlour at the corner of Newgate Street and South Church Road taken in the 1930s. It was opened by Gennaro Rossi who came to England in 1908 from a village near Cassino in Italy. The cafe was originally the Waterloo Hotel, then the Auckland Cocoa Rooms and was later altered by the Rossi family to become a typical coffee bar. Teenagers gathered there, romances blossomed and today many couples remember it with great affection as their meeting place. Rossi's moved premises to the Market Place and their famous coffee and delicious food is now served by the third and fourth generations of the family.

South Church Road, c.1970, showing Raine's tobacconist's shop, the Alma Hotel and Appleton's fish shop. Through the Archway was Hull's coachbuilders, later a taxi firm.

The Girl's County School, Bishop Auckland, c.1950.

The gymnasium of the girl's school. It is now part of the King James I comprehensive school.

Girl's at the school demonstrate a uniform of gymslips and baggy stockings.

The old united Methodist Church in Newgate Street, c.1890.

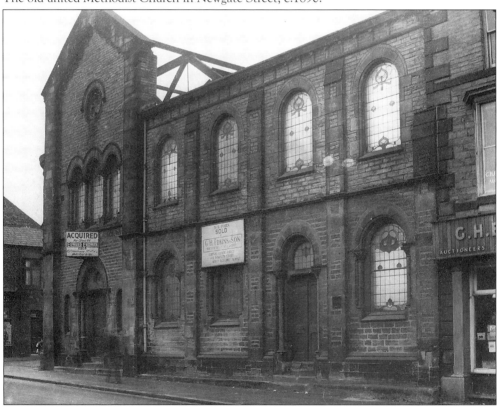

Demolition of the church, c.1970. Proceeds of the sale of the land went to build a new church on Woodhouse Close Estate.

The view on leaving Bishop Auckland railway station, c.1910. Originally South Road, it is now part of Newgate Street.

The Wear Valley Hotel, c.1960. Near the railway station, it was popular with commercial travellers. Brotherton's music shop next door was established in 1842.

A modern picture of the former Green Tree Hotel in Cockton Hill Road built in 1900.

The crest above the door of the former Green Tree Hotel.

The present Lady Eden Day Unit was the cottage hospital, opened 8th September 1899 by Lord Roseberry. Lady Eden was the mother of Sir Anthony Eden, a former Prime Minister.

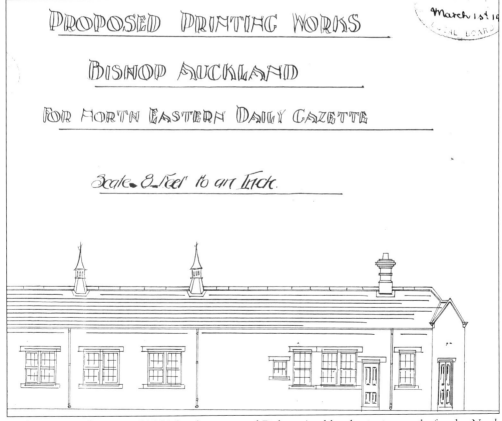

A planning application of 1904 for the proposed Bishop Auckland printing works for the *North Eastern Daily Gazette*.

Central Methodist Church, Cockton Hill Road. Most of the town's original Methodist churches have now amalgamated into this church.

Cockton Hill Road, 1910. These Victorian houses, built on the common grazingland of Bishop Auckland, were much sought after by the town's tradespeople.

The toll house at Cabin Gate, c.1700, was on the road from Bishop Auckland to Barnard Castle.

Escomb's Saxon Church, c.1980, is one of the oldest churches in the country still in regular use. Some of the stone for the seventh century building came from the Roamn fort at Vinovium.

St. Andew's Church taken from East Lychgate, c.1960. Although well away from the present town centre, this ancient church is the parish church of Bishop Auckland.

East Deanery, South Church. Now a popular restaurant, this building once housed monks turned out of Durham Cathedral because of their failure to conform to regulations.

Two
Transport

The Bishop Auckland to Stanhope coach, c.1880, ran a daily service from what is now the Post Chaise Hotel in Bishop Auckland Market Place.

Mr. John Howe of West Auckland proudly shows off his motor car, c.1900.

Bishop Auckland's horse drawn fire engine was stationed behind the Sun Inn, High Bondgate. It was used until the 1930s when it was replaced by *Bulldog Drummond*, a converted Rover car.

An Elgey's lorry of the 1920s. Joseph Elgey's timber yard in Railway Street specialised in the manufacture of tool handles for the mining industry.

A load of Lingford's products ready for shipment to Barbados in June 1946, one of the first peace-time exports. During the Second World War the baking powder firm also made dried eggs and dried milk.

This United bus ran a frequent service in the 1920s. Boothroyd's Opticians still practice in Bishop Auckland on the same site where Alfred George Boothroyd opened his business as a watchmaker and jeweller in 1907. He later specialised in optics.

Bishop Auckland's first double decker bus took to the streets in 1913. It seemed to be popular with no room on top or inside.

Mr. Railton, one of the last greengocers to sell his goods from a horse and cart in the streets of Bishop Auckland, c.1970.

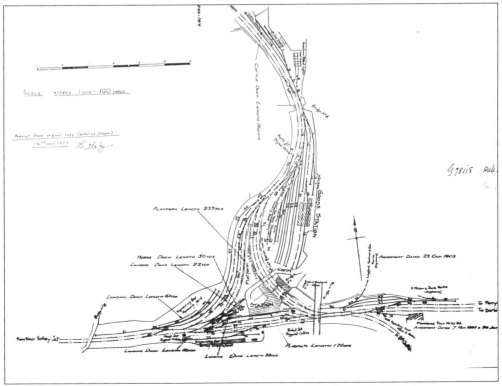

The 1924 lay-out of Bishop Auckland railway station showing the rare triangular junction.

The interior of Bishop Auckland East Signal Box, 22nd October 1980. The megaphone on the shelf was used by signalmen to speak to drivers.

BRITISH RAILWAYS

SUMMARY OF
PROPOSED EXCURSIONS
FOR
WOMEN'S ORGANISATIONS
FROM THE
MIDDLESBROUGH
WEST HARTLEPOOL
and DARLINGTON AREAS
1963

Dear Madam,
I have pleasure in bringing to your notice suggestions for outings for the spring and early summer, 1963. It will be noticed that certain new features have been introduced.

Each excursion provides for a rail journey in modern tourist coaching stock, good meals in both directions, attractive sightseeing tours, all designed to give the maximum of comfort and entertainment to members of the parties with the minimum of trouble to organisers.

The full programme will, of course, be carried out only if sufficient support is forthcoming and it will be greatly to your advantage to indicate your wishes early and so secure accommodation. I recommend therefore, that you make a provisional booking on the form enclosed before the end of December, earlier if possible, and confirm your final numbers nearer the date of the outing.

I hope that this folder will be helpful to you and your members in planning your 1963 programme. If you wish I shall be pleased to arrange for my representative to call on you to discuss your plans in further detail.

Yours faithfully,

District Commercial Superintendent
MIDDLESBROUGH

Summer excursions for women from Bishop Auckland in 1963 included trips to Paris for three days for £ 29 10s, all inclusive.

Diesel E50269 and 56067 departing from Bishop Auckland on 4th April 1970.

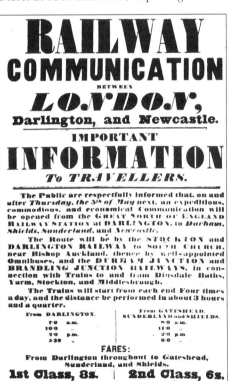

A poster from 1842 advertising a new rail/omnibus link between Darlington and Newcastle calling at South Church, Bishop Auckland.

The front cover of the *The Rokeby Polka* composed by William Crawford, station master at Bishop Auckland in 1881. His daughters ran the station buffet.

Bishop Auckland railway station in the 1950s. The station was lit by gas until its demolition because of a long term agreement.

Sandy Boyd's bridge, the railway bridge which crossed Princes Street until 1977. It was named after the owner of the Masonic Music Hall which stood on the cleared space to the left under the bridge.

Bone Mill Bank at South Church, c.1950s. The engine crossing the bridge is travelling from Darlington to Bishop Auckland.

Sir Vincent Raven designed this B16 class locomotive seen here at Bishop Auckland station taking passengers on a special tour.

A driver's view of the bridge carrying Newgate Street into Cockton Hill Road, 8th January 1950.

The lay-out of Bishop Auckland railway station in the 1950s.

60004, a streamlined A4 Pacific used to haul express passenger trains at Bishop Auckland on 19th September 1965. The most famous of this class, *Mallard*, achieved 126 m.p.h. on 3rd July 1938. It was considered to be the masterpiece of designer Sir Nigel Gresley.

Signalmen J. Stephenson and F. Tennick changing duty at the towering north signal box in June 1968.

63398, another of Sir Vincent Raven's designs, this Q6 class heavy main line freight engine is seen here working in snowy conditions. Seventy of these locomotives were built at Darlington upto 1919 and the last fifty were built by Armstrong Whitworth and Co.

60

Bridges were a major feature of Bishop Auckland railway station because of the complexity of the track layout. This footbridge is well remembered by passengers who used the station.

A G5 class light passenger locomotive designed by Wilson Worsdell and built at Darlington between 1894 and 1901. The Co-op bakery is on the left behind No. 4 platform.

Station master Mr. Coomber with a group of Bishop Auckland railway staff, c.1961. Left to right: G. Sparling, Luke Raine, Mr. Parvin, Mr. Coomber, Mr. Mortimer, J. Buddin, Mr. Firbank, -?- .

Civic leaders from Stockton, Darlington, Sedgefield, Durham County and Wear Valley attending the renaming ceremony of Escomb station to Witton Park station on Sunday, 25th August 1991.

Three
Auckland Castle

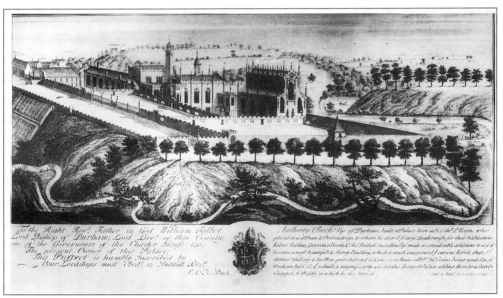

Auckland Castle at the time of Bishop William Talbot (1722-30). The clock tower was later demolished and the clock transferred to the new gatehouse built by Bishop Trevor where it can still be seen.

The Gateway to Auckland Castle and the Bishop's Park, c.1950. The gate was built by Bishop Richard Trevor in the eighteenth century.

Now used as offices and flats, this building, just inside the gate, was once a flax mill.

The drive from the gate to Auckland Castle, c. 1930. The drive was created when the gate was built. Thousands of tons of soil were used to raise the natural slope down to the river Gaunless.

The stone screen in front of the castle, c. 1930. It was erected by Bishop Shute Barrington (1791-1826).

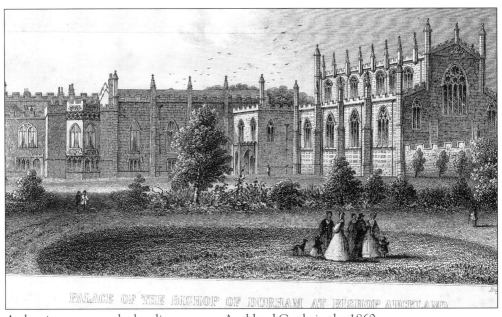

PALACE OF THE BISHOP OF DURHAM AT BISHOP AUCKLAND

A chatting group on the bowling green at Auckland Castle in the 1860s.

The gardener tends to the immaculate lawns outside St. Peter's Chapel (right) and the Throne Room (left).

The rear entrance guardroom of Auckland Castle dating from the fourteenth century with the pillars of the castle stables in the foreground.

Auckland Castle from the former stable yard, 1980. The Scotland wing (right), built in the fourteenth century by Bishop Walter Skirlaw, had two uses - the upper floor was a walking gallery and the lower floor was used to house Scottish prisoners.

A sixteenth century stone carving of the coat of arms of the See of Durham in the walls of Auckland Castle. Included in the surrounding stonework are a camel and a jester.

The work of a sixteenth century stonemason at Auckland Castle - a workman giving his collegue a ride in the wheelbarrow !

The ornate wooden screen at the entrance to St. Peter's Chapel was installed by Bishop John Cosin in the 1660s. Screens like this, favoured by 'High Church' Anglicans, can be seen as a reaction against Oliver Cromwell and the Puritans who had previously been in power and who liked their churches very plain. The work on the screen was done by two carpenters who were paid 40s (£2) per yard for the job. St. Peter's Chapel is the largest private chapel in England. Built in the twelfth century by Bishop Hugh de Puiset as a grand banquet hall, it was converted to a chapel by Bishop Cosin after the restoration of the monarchy. The pillars are sandstone and Frosterley marble, a local Weardale limestone filled with fossils dating back over 300 million years. Bishop Cosin's tomb, in the floor in the centre, is also made from Frosterley marble. The window above the altar depicts scenes from the life of St. Peter and other windows in the chapel tell the story of early christianity in north east Enlgand. They were installed by Bishop Joseph Barber Lightfoot and when the work was completed, in 1888, 57 Anglican bishops from all over the world attended the re-dedication ceremony. Around the walls are the coats of arms of many of the Bishops of Durham.

St. Peter's Chapel, Auckland Castle.

The orante wooden ceiling of St. Peter's Chapel at Auckland Castle with the coat of arms of Bishop Cosin and the See of Durham.

This marble monument to Bishop Trevor which stands in the ante-chapel of St. Peter's is the work of the sculptor Joseph Nollekens.

The Throne Room at Auckland Castle, c. 1890. The Throne Room was built by Bishop Anthony Bek in the fourteenth century and was among those rooms at the castle redesigned by architect James Wyatt for Bishop Barrington in the early nineteenth century. Above the throne at the far end of the room is Bishop Barrington's coat of arms showing the sword and coronet unique to the Prince Bishops of Durham. Around the walls are portraits of many former Bishops of Durham. Here the Throne Room is very over furnished, typical of Victorian times, but most of the furniture was sold by auction in the 1930s and today visitors have unrestricted and much more impressive view of the room and its portraits.

Cardinal Thomas Wolsey, Bishop of Durham from 1523 to 1529, never entered the Diocese. He was appointed by Henry VIII to gain access to the wealth of the See which at the time was considerable.

Cuthbert Tunstall was the last Roman Catholic Bishop of Durham (1530-1559).

74

James Pilkington, the first Protestant Bishop of Durham, from 1561 to 1576, is accused by history of selling off church treasures and using the proceeds for himself and family.

John Cosin was Bishop of Durham from 1660 to 1672. Appointed at the age of 66, he did a lot of work to repair and improve Auckland Castle after the Commonwealth period.

Engraved for Hutchinson's History & Antiquities of Durham.

NATHANIEL LORD CREWE.

Bishop of Durham.

Nathaniel, Lord Crewe, was the longest serving Bishop of Durham - for 48 years from 1674 to 1722. He installed the Father Schmidt organ in Auckland Castle and left money in his will to teach the poor boys of Bishop Auckland to read and write.

Richard Trevor, Bishop of Durham from 1752 to 1771.

William Van Mildert, Bishop
of Durham from 1826 to 1836,
was the last of the Prince
Bishops. He helped to found
Durham Univerity and gave
up Durham Castle to become
University college, making his
home permanently at
Auckland Castle.

Bishop Edward Maltby (1836-
1856) was a generous benefactor
to the poor of Bishop Auckland,
building an alms house in the
Market Place.

Bishop Brooke Foss Westcott (1889-1901) is remembered as the coal miners' bishop for his intervention on their behalf in disputes with the owners.

Bishop Westcott relaxes with his dog, Mephistopheles, in the grounds of Auckland Castle on St. Peter's Day in 1894.

A family group at Auckland Castle at the turn of the century.

Bishop Auckland and District Endeavour Council pose for a picture during a visit to Auckland Castle in November 1908.

Bishop Joseph Barber Lightfoot (1879-1889) with 'Lightfoot's Lambs' in 1883. These young men came to Auckland Castle to study with the Bishop and formed a brotherhood which lasted even though they dispersed to all corners of the world - from Argentina to the Punjab, South Australia to Japan. They kept in touch with each other through the *Auckland Chronicle*, their own magazine. In the issue presented here one former scholar, by then Bishop of Argentina and Eastern South America, tells of a typical Latin American Sunday, with race meetings, street processions and fireworks; another writes from Manitoba in Canada telling how the ladies at his church send clothes to the Red Indians; and yet another describes his work in South Africa among the inmates of Transvaal Gaol. Recollections of Bishop Lightfoot tell of his delight in a joke, 'laughing till the tears ran down his cheeks', and of another, less amusing day, when the Bishop ended up with his clothes torn and his hands bleeding after rescuing his favourite collie 'Dugald' from an attack by a mastiff.

The Auckland Chronicle, the magazine of 'Lightfoot's Lambs', July 1910 edition.

The Bishop's Coachman at Auckland Castle in the late 1800s.

The river Gaunless flowing through the Bishop's Park, c. 1950. The park contained many fine old trees.

The flower show in the Bishop's Park, c. 1870.

The footbridge that used to span the Gaunless in the Bishop's Park, c. 1910.

The wishing temple that used to stand in the Bishop's Park, c. 1910. A favourite spot to visit on a walk, it was built from stones which had formed the butter cross and the town pant, demolished in 1861 for the Town Hall to be built.

The Deerhouse in the Bishop's Park was built by Bishop Trevor in 1760 as shelter for the fallow deer which roamed the 800 acre parkland.

An aerial view of Auckland Castle.

Four

Entertainment

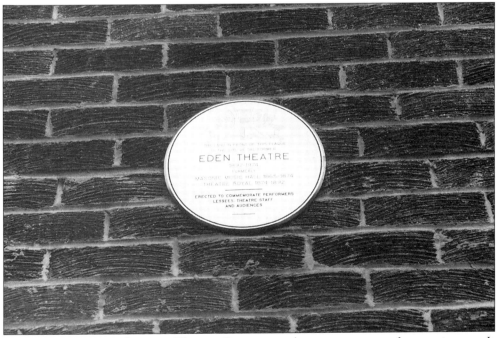

The commemorative plaque at Theatre Corner records over a century of entertainment. It marks the site of the Masonic Music Hall (1865-74), the Theatre Royal (1874-92) and the Eden Theatre (1892-1974).

The tombstone of John Borrowdale in St. Andrew's chuchyard at South Church. John, the town constable in 1812, was an enthusiastic amateur actor.

Theatre Corner, c. 1910. Left of the building, near the bridge, is the Eden Theatre. At the front of the picture is the Theatre Hotel.

Charles Draycott was manager of the Eden Theatre from 1916 until he died on 7th October 1917.

Muriel Draycott took over the running of the theatre when her husband died. She stayed there until 1921.

The most popular ever performed in Bishop Auckland - Wilson Barrett's *The Sign of the Cross*. This programme was for the preformance of October 1902 at the Eden Theatre.

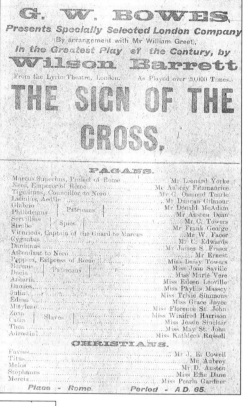

The oldest surviving programme of the Eden Theatre, for Wednesday 10th January 1894. It was a benefit for Arthur Jefferson, the father of film comedian Stan Laurel. 'Mrs Cregan' is played by Stan's mother.

Arthur Jefferson, Stan Laurel and Arthur's second wife, Venetia, at a dockside reunion in 1935. Arthur Jefferson, an actor manager, ran the Theatre Royal, Bishop Auckland from 1889. In 1892 he changed the name to the Eden Theatre, the Edens of nearby Windlestone Hall being the local nobility. He continued to run the theatre until 1896 when he left to go to North Shields and Glasgow. He returned to Bishop Auckland in 1922 to run the Eden Theatre again until 1925 when he moved to London to run a theatrical agency.

Arthur Stanley Jefferson, better known as Stan Laurel, with Oliver Hardy. Stan lived in Princes Street and Waldron Street, Bishop Auckland, as a young child. The family moved away but he returned to the town in 1902 as a boarder at King James I School.

Programme for the grand opening of the Hippodrome, Railway Street, on Monday 6th December 1909. Top of the bill was Lil Hawthorne, the famous London comedienne.

Lil Hawthorne played a crucial part in the capture of the infamous Dr. Crippen murderer. She alerted the authorities to the fact that her friend, Belle Ellemore, was missing. Dr. Crippen had killed Belle, his wife, and was arrested as he tried to flee the country with his girlfriend.

The Hippodrome, Bishop Auckland, c. 1980. It opened as a variety theatre in 1909, then became a cinema, and finally houses a bingo hall.

A silk programme for the grand opening of the Eden Theatre, Bishop Auckland, under new ownership on Christmas Eve 1902.

Eden Theatre
BISHOP AUCKLAND

THE AUDITORIUM

Programme

PRICE TWOPENCE

The auditorium of the Eden Theatre as it was in 1927 after its refurbishment.

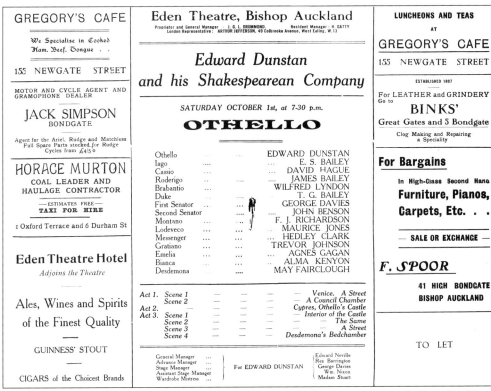

Eden Theatre, Bishop Auckland

Proprietor and General Manager - J. G. L. DRUMMOND.   Resident Manager : H. GATTY
London Representative : ARTHUR JEFFERSON, 49 Colbrooke Avenue, West Ealing. W.13

Edward Dunstan
and his Shakespearean Company

SATURDAY OCTOBER 1st, at 7-30 p.m.

OTHELLO

Othello	... ...	EDWARD DUNSTAN
Iago	....	... E. S. BAILEY
Cassio	...	... DAVID HAGUE
Roderigo	.. ....	.... JAMES BAILEY
Brabantio	...	WILFRED LYNDON
Duke	... .	... T. G. BAILEY
First Senator	.. ...	GEORGE DAVIES
Second Senator	...	... JOHN BENSON
Montano	... ...	F. J. RICHARDSON
Lodeveco	... ...	... MAURICE JONES
Messenger	... ...	... HEDLEY CLARK
Gratiano	... ...	TREVOR JOHNSON
Emelia	... ...	... AGNES GAGAN
Bianca	.. ...	.. ALMA KENYON
Desdemona	....	MAY FAIRCLOUGH

Act 1.	Scene 1	—	—	—	—	Venice. A Street
	Scene 2	—	—	—	—	A Council Chamber
Act 2.						Cypres, Othello's Castle
Act 3.	Scene 1	—	—	—	—	Interior of the Castle
	Scene 2	—	—	—	—	The Same
	Scene 3	—	—	—	—	A Street
	Scene 4	—	—	—		Desdemona's Bedchamber

General Manager	...			Edward Neville
Advance Manager	...		For EDWARD DUNSTAN	Rex Barrington
Stage Manager	...			George Davies
Assistant Stage Manager	...			Wm. Nixon
Wardrobe Mistress	...			Madam Stuart

Theatre programme of the 1920s. Edward Dunstan made frequent visits to Bishop Auckland with his Shakesperean company.

FOR BOYS AND GIRLS.

The ROYAL STAGE CIRCUS
At the Eden Theatre

will give a

Special Matinee on Saturday, at 2-30

Prices for Children : 3d., 6d., 8d. and 1/-

Printed at the Press of G W Budd, Ltd., Bishop Auckland.

The Eden Theatre even staged circuses. Stage hands remember them for the smell they left behind.

BEAUTY THE ONLY PERFORMING ZEBRA IN THE WORLD AT ROYAL CIRCUS.

The Royal Circus involved the zebra *Beauty*. *Beauty* was a bit of beast. Apparently she kicked down the dressing room door.

Jours Always Alpa

THE ONLY TROUPE OF PERFORMING GEESE IN THE WORLD

It is not recorded what mischief the performing geese got up to.

The Sam Livesey's company performed melodramas at the Eden Theatre in the early 1900s. *The Village Blacksmith* was one of their most famous plays.

The Village Blacksmith.

Mr. SAM LIVESEY
— as —
THE BLACKSMITH.

Sam Livesey's wife acted with the company under the stage name Miss Maggie Edwards.

Dr. Walford Bodie, c. 1905, performed at
the Eden as the 'Electric Wizard'.

Cometa, the Egytian illusionist, was another
speciality act at the theatre in the early years
of the century.

Musical comedy was all the rage in 1914. The Eden Theatre presented many of the best known productions of the time including *San Toy*.

Frank E. Franks, the best remembered pantomime artist to appear at the Eden Theatre between the wars.

Ivy Duke, a film star sex symbol who turned to straight theatre, appeared at the Eden in November 1926.

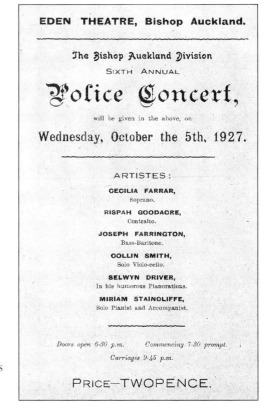

EDEN THEATRE, Bishop Auckland.

The Bishop Auckland Division

SIXTH ANNUAL

Police Concert,

will be given in the above, on

Wednesday, October the 5th, 1927.

ARTISTES:

CECILIA FARRAR,
Soprano.

RISPAH GOODACRE,
Contralto.

JOSEPH FARRINGTON,
Bass-Baritone.

COLLIN SMITH,
Solo Violo-cello.

SELWYN DRIVER,
In his humorous Pianorations.

MIRIAM STAINCLIFFE,
Solo Pianist and Accompanist.

Doors open 6-30 p.m.   Commencing 7-30 prompt.
Carriages 9-45 p.m.

PRICE—TWOPENCE.

The Eden Theatre was used by local as well as professional groups. This police concert was preformed on Wednesday 5th October 1927.

The Knights of the Golden Horn held a special night at the Eden Theatre in 1927.

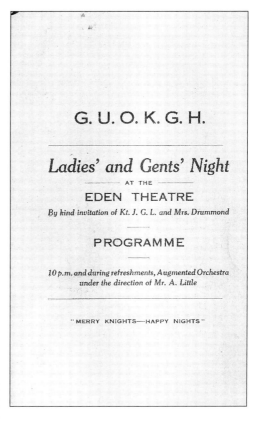

G. U. O. K. G. H.

Ladies' and Gents' Night
——— AT THE ———
EDEN THEATRE
By kind invitation of Kt. J. G. L. and Mrs. Drummond

PROGRAMME

*10 p.m. and during refreshments, Augmented Orchestra
under the direction of Mr. A. Little*

"MERRY KNIGHTS—HAPPY NIGHTS"

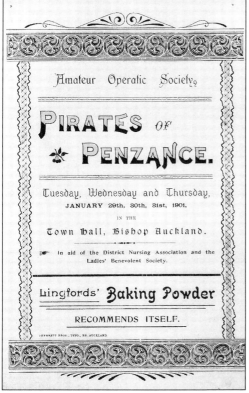

Amateur Operatic Society.

PIRATES OF PENZANCE.

Tuesday, Wednesday and Thursday,
JANUARY 29th, 30th, 31st, 1901,
IN THE
Town Hall, Bishop Auckland.

In aid of the District Nursing Association and the Ladies' Benevolent Society.

Lingfords' Baking Powder

RECOMMENDS ITSELF.

The Bishop Auckland Amateur Operatic Society staged *Pirates of Penzance* in Bishop Auckland Town Hall in January 1901. Founded in 1898, the society disbanded during the wars and reformed in 1946.

Mrs Hetty Sutton (nee Trussler) was associated with the Eden Theatre bar for 38 years. She first worked there on leaving school and later returned with her husband Andrew. She was landlady druing the 1930s, 40s, and 50s.

Hetty with regulars in the bar, c.1938.

A 1921 example of local firms using the
Eden Theatre programmes to advertise.

Despite the claim that Lingfords Baking
Powder recommended itself, the firm still felt
the need to advertise.

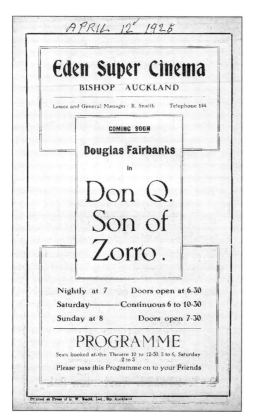

Eden Super Cinema
BISHOP AUCKLAND

Lessee and General Manager : R. Snaith   Telephone 144

COMING SOON

Douglas Fairbanks

in

Don Q. Son of Zorro.

Nightly at 7   Doors open at 6-30
Saturday————Continuous 6 to 10-30
Sunday at 8   Doors open 7-30

PROGRAMME

Seats booked at the Theatre 10 to 12-30, 2 to 6, Saturday 2 to 5
Please pass this Programme on to your Friends

Printed at Press of G. W. Radd, Ltd., Bp. Auckland

A programme for the Eden Super Cinema, 12 April 1925. At this time the Eden operated as part theatre, part cinema.

GF 8930

BISHOP AUCKLAND ENTERTAINMENTS.

Coronation Month Souvenir Programme.

MAY, 1937.

Theatre and Cinema owner J. G. L. Drummond produced a monthly guide to the Eden Theatre, Hippodrome and King's Hall cinemas. This coronation souvenir edition was published in May 1937.

Front of house staff of the Eden Theatre, c.1950. Mrs Drummond, the owner's wife, is seen fifth from the left.

President: J.G.L. DRUMMOND

Bishop Auckland Rotary Club.

President's Victory Year Ball

Kings Restaurant, Bishop Auckland,
Monday, December 10th, 1945.

J.G.L. Drummond, as President of Bishop Auckland Rotary Club, December 1945. He was at one time Chairman of the Urban District Council.

103

The end of the Eden Theatre in 1974. The bulldozers moved in to make way for a new road through the town. Built by Sandy Boyd in the 1870s for melodramas, it was extended by Arthur Jefferson and renamed the Eden Theatre in 1892. Straight plays, comedies, opera and pantomimes were all performed to packed houses. But when cinema and television came, provincial theatre died. The Eden showed films but newer places were more successful. It degenerated to third rate variety and finally became a bingo hall, but it was old and tired and could no longer pull in the crowds. Now it is gone it is mourned by many.

Five

People

Pupils of Cockton Hill Council Girls School dressed in their best for their annual school picture, c.1920.

Briton the horse pulled handcarts up steep Newton Cap Bank into Bishop Auckland for a penny a time. The owner is William Snowball, left, who lived with his family in Thompson Street, c.1890.

The miners of Newton Cap with their lodge banner in 1924.

Robert Archibald Dougals Gresley, the last Borough Bailiff of Bishop Auckland, 1851. Born in 1794 in Worcestershire, he was educated at Rugby and became a solicitor. A nephew by marriage to Bishop Van Mildert, he came to Bishop Auckland as his secretary and bailiff and lived in the Market Place near Auckland Castle's gate. He presided at the Petty Sessions held at the Shepherds Inn, Fore Bondgate, on the first and third Thursday of every month until his retirement in 1856 when he moved to live in Droitwich. He died on 13th February 1885, aged 90.

Thomas Morgan, c.1870. A Welshman, he came to the Bishop Auckland area when the Bolckow and Vaughan ironworks were established at Witton Park. A talented singer, he was a valued member of the Bishop Auckland Musical Society until his sudden death in 1880.

Belgian refugees at Witton Park in 1914.

Joseph Lingford, 1911, from an oil painting by Henry Daniel. Born in Nottingham, Lingford
(1829-1918) started making his famous baking powder there. In 1888 his business movd to
Durham Street, Bishop Auckland, to be run by his son Ernest. A Quaker who took an active
part in civic life, Joseph lived in Bishop Auckland for many years. On 27th October 1911 the
people of the town presented him with a life-size portrait which was hung in the Town Hall.

Bishop Auckland's main war memorial, c.1922. To erect it money was raised through the Eden Theatre Heroes Memorial Fund. Originally near the railway station, it was moved to the Market Place in the 1980s.

Men of the 6th Battalion of the Durham Light Infantry at Ypres, 24 May 1915.

Another war memorial in St. Andrew's churchyard at South Church was erected by church members.

The 6th Battalion of the Durham Light Infantry was raised in Bishop Auckland. Many local men joined up never to return, among them Private Perry (front right).

Mine rescue team, c.1910. With many coal mines in the area a highly trained rescue team was essential when accidents occured. Note the canaries used to detect gases and the breathing apparatus worn by the team.

An air raid warden practises his first aid skills, c.1941. Incidents were staged involving volunteers.

Preparations for a carnival parade, c.1900. The entrance to the drill hall of the 2nd Battalion Durham Light Infantry is in the background.

Staff of Doggarts department store at their annual dance in 1933.

A workroom at the West Auckland Clothing Company factory, c.1950. Women in the area still have a high reputation for their skills in clothing manufacture.

Lunch hour break at the clothing factory, c.1950.

Men of the area combine their skills to build St. Helen's, Auckland's community service centre.

The men take time off to pose for an official picture.

Pupils at Cockton Hill School, c.1905. This early photograph shows the styles of dress - note the boys' clogs.

Class 9 of Cockton Hill Girls School in 1922. Maggie Morgan (front row, right) treasured this picture of her classmates.

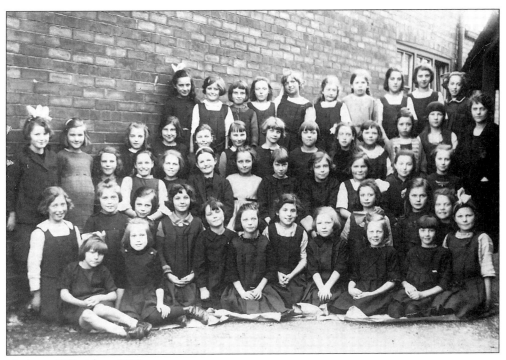

Cockton Hill girls, c.1920.

Mothers had obviously worked hard making fairy costumes for the Cockton Hill Girls play.

The Brownies, with Brown Owl, pose for the photographer.

Bishop Auckland Girl Guides in the 1920s.

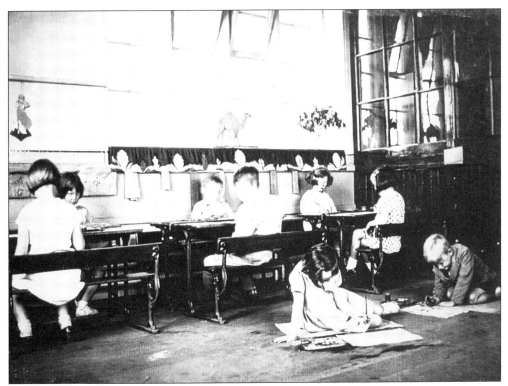

Children at their lessons in Escomb village school, c.1950.

More lessons at Escomb village school. It has since been refurbished.

The winning team when Bishop Auckland won the F.A. Amateur Cup for the sixth time, beating Wibledon 2 - 1 in a replay at Stamford Bridge on 20th April 1935. The scorers were A. Wilson (left, middle row) and R. Bryan (right, middle row).

The cup winning Bishop Auckland team of 1939 beat Willington 3 - 0 at Roker Park Sunderland. This was the seventh time Bishop Auckland won the Amateur Cup. The *Two Blues* notched up ten wins before the competition was abandoned. Second from the right is Bob Paisley who went on to become manager of Liverpool.

A crowd at Bishop Auckland's Kingsway ground in the 1930s. The men spent their Saturday afternoons here but during the week were more likely to be at the building at the back - the labour exchange. The area suffered very badly during the depression.

The men's swimming team at Eldon open air baths in 1913. The baths, which stood in the valley below Black Boy Pit, were built by miners for the community.

Jack Hatfield, champion of England exhibition at the Eldon Gala.

George Burt (Baths Manager) with junior champion Arthur Mothersdale (left), Eldon Baths 1912.

Members of the Auckland Touring Club on a Sunday run to Stanhope in the 1970s. The club was founded in 1962 and Bob and Dorothy Goundry who ran it for many years encouraged hundreds of young people to enjoy cycling as a sport and a hobby. These were not fair weather cyclists. They went out on their Sunday runs in hail, rain and snow. Regular rides included 50 miles in four hours, 100 miles in eight hours and *King of the Mountain* rides over the wild and isolated fell roads of Weardale. The Touring Club did not just confine its activities to local runs. They also toured Scotland, Ireland, Austria, Italy and Germany.

The Auckland Touring Club members pause for refreshments and a chat with fellow cyclists during a tour of Austria.

The Touring Club members were always encouraged to check their bearings. Here they are doing some map reading in Austria.

Members of the Cockton Hill Bowling Club with some of their trophies.

Ladies of the Cockton Hill Bowling Club.

Red Alligator, the 1968 Grand National winner and his local jockey Brain Fletcher, were hailed as heroes when they returned home to Bishop Auckland. Naturally the punters were pleased - they had backed him at odds of 100 - 7. Brain Fletcher had two other memorable Grand National wins, both on the legendary *Red Rum*. *Red Alligator* had a pub named after him at South Church near his trainer, Denys Smith's stables.

Red Alligator and jockey Brain Fletcher get a Town Hall reception in 1968.

The pub sign that commemorates Bishop Auckland's proudest racing moment.

No book on the history of Bishop Auckland would be complete without paying tribute to two men who have done so much to stimulate interest in it - Derek Hebden and the late Frank Hutchinson. Derek, a former journalist, came from Middlesborough to Bishop Auckland in the 1950s with the *Evening Gazette*. He worked for the *Northern Echo* and was for many years the chief reporter of the area's weekly paper, the *Auckland Chronicle*. A former Chairman of Bishop Auckland Urban Distrct Council, he not only involved himself in the current isues of the day but also researched the area's past. His books include *Bishop Auckland Remembered*, *When Bishop Auckland was a Village* and *Bishop Auckland 100 Years Ago*. He has also written books about West Auckland and St. Helens, Witton Park and the infamous child murderer Mary Ann Cotton. Derek is now retired.

The late Frank Hutchinson, pictured here in 1931, was a founder of the Auckland Amenities Association which did so much to encourage pride in the town and an appreciation of its history. Frank believed in recording facts of the day for tomorrow's historians. He took pictures of buildings under threat of demolition and of places likely to be changed. His records are already proving useful and in the future they can only become more so.

Stock List

(Titles are listed according to the pre-1974 county boundaries)

BERKSHIRE

Wantage
Irene Hancock
ISBN 0-7524-0146 7

CARDIGANSHIRE

Aberaeron and Mid Ceredigion
William Howells
ISBN 0-7524-0106-8

CHESHIRE

Ashton-under-Lyne and Mossley
Alice Lock
ISBN 0-7524-0164-5

Around Bebington
Pat O'Brien
ISBN 0-7524-0121-1

Crewe
Brian Edge
ISBN 0-7524-0052-5

Frodsham and Helsby
Frodsham and District Local History Group
ISBN 0-7524-0161-0

Macclesfield Silk
Moira Stevenson and Louanne Collins
ISBN 0-7524-0315 X

Marple
Steve Cliffe
ISBN 0-7524-0316-8

Runcorn
Bert Starkey
ISBN 0-7524-0025-8

Warrington
Janice Hayes
ISBN 0-7524-0040-1

West Kirby to Hoylake
Jim O'Neil
ISBN 0-7524-0024-X

Widnes
Anne Hall and the Widnes Historical Society
ISBN 0-7524-0117-3

CORNWALL

Padstow
Malcolm McCarthy
ISBN 0-7524-0033-9

St Ives Bay
Jonathan Holmes
ISBN 0-7524-0186-6

COUNTY DURHAM

Bishop Auckland
John Land
ISBN 0-7524-0312-5

Around Shildon
Vera Chapman
ISBN 0-7524-0115-7

CUMBERLAND

Carlisle
Dennis Perriam
ISBN 0-7524-0166-1

DERBYSHIRE

Around Alfreton
Alfreton and District Heritage Trust
ISBN 0-7524-0041-X

Barlborough, Clowne, Creswell and Whitwell
Les Yaw
ISBN 0-7524-0031-2

Around Bolsover
Bernard Haigh
ISBN 0-7524-0021-5

Around Derby
Alan Champion and Mark Edworthy
ISBN 0-7524-0020-7

Long Eaton
John Barker
ISBN 0-7524-0110-6

Ripley and Codnor
David Buxton
ISBN 0-7524-0042-8

Shirebrook
Geoff Sadler
ISBN 0-7524-0028-2

Shirebrook: A Second Selection
Geoff Sadler
ISBN 0-7524-0317-6

DEVON

Brixham
Ted Gosling and Lyn Marshall
ISBN 0-7524-0037-1

Around Honiton
Les Berry and Gerald Gosling
ISBN 0-7524-0175-0

Around Newton Abbot
Les Berry and Gerald Gosling
ISBN 0-7524-0027-4

Around Ottery St Mary
Gerald Gosling and Peter Harris
ISBN 0-7524-0030-4

Around Sidmouth
Les Berry and Gerald Gosling
ISBN 0-7524-0137-8

DORSET

Around Uplyme and Lyme Regis
Les Berry and Gerald Gosling
ISBN 0-7524-0044-4

ESSEX

Braintree and Bocking
John and Sandra Adlam and Mark Charlton
ISBN 0-7524-0129-7

Ilford
Ian Dowling and Nick Harris
ISBN 0-7524-0050-9

Ilford: A Second Selection
Ian Dowling and Nick Harris
ISBN 0-7524-0320-6

Saffron Walden
Jean Gumbrell
ISBN 0-7524-0176-9

GLAMORGAN

Around Bridgend
Simon Eckley
ISBN 0-7524-0189-0

Caerphilly
Simon Eckley
ISBN 0-7524-0194-7

Around Kenfig Hill and Pyle
Keith Morgan
ISBN 0-7524-0314-1

The County Borough of Merthyr Tydfil
Carolyn Jacob, Stephen Done and Simon Eckley
ISBN 0-7524-0012-6

Mountain Ash, Penrhiwceiber and Abercynon
Bernard Baldwin and Harry Rogers
ISBN 0-7524-0114-9

Pontypridd
Simon Eckley
ISBN 0-7524-0017-7

Rhondda
Simon Eckley and Emrys Jenkins
ISBN 0-7524-0028-2

Rhondda: A Second Selection
Simon Eckley and Emrys Jenkins
ISBN 0-7524-0308-7

Roath, Splott, and Adamsdown
Roath Local History Society
ISBN 0-7524-0199-8

GLOUCESTERSHIRE

Barnwood, Hucclecote and Brockworth
Alan Sutton
ISBN 0-7524-0000-2

Forest to Severn
Humphrey Phelps
ISBN 0-7524-0008-8

Filton and the Flying Machine
Malcolm Hall
ISBN 0-7524-0171-8

Gloster Aircraft Company
Derek James
ISBN 0-7524-0038-X

The City of Gloucester
Jill Voyce
ISBN 0-7524-0306-0

Around Nailsworth and Minchinhampton from the Conway Collection
Howard Beard
ISBN 0-7524-0048-7

Around Newent
Tim Ward
ISBN 0-7524-0003-7

Stroud: Five Stroud Photographers
Howard Beard, Peter Harris and Wilf Merrett
ISBN 0-7524-0305-2

HAMPSHIRE

Gosport
Ian Edelman
ISBN 0-7524-0300-1

Winchester from the Sollars Collection
John Brimfield
ISBN 0-7524-0173-4

HEREFORDSHIRE

Ross-on-Wye
Tom Rigby and Alan Sutton
ISBN 0-7524-0002-9

HERTFORDSHIRE

Buntingford
Philip Plumb
ISBN 0-7524-0170-X

Hampstead Garden Suburb
Mervyn Miller
ISBN 0-7524-0319-2

Hemel Hempstead
Eve Davis
ISBN 0-7524-0167-X

Letchworth
Mervyn Miller
ISBN 0-7524-0318-4

Welwyn Garden City
Angela Eserin
ISBN 0-7524-0133-5

KENT

Hythe
Joy Melville and Angela Lewis-Johnson
ISBN 0-7524-0169-6

North Thanet Coast
Alan Kay
ISBN 0-7524-0112-2

Shorts Aircraft
Mike Hooks
ISBN 0-7524-0193-9

LANCASHIRE

Lancaster and the Lune Valley
Robert Alston
ISBN 0-7524-0015-0

Morecambe Bay
Robert Alston
ISBN 0-7524-0163-7

Manchester
Peter Stewart
ISBN 0-7524-0103-3

LINCOLNSHIRE

Louth
David Cuppleditch
ISBN 0-7524-0172-6

Stamford
David Gerard
ISBN 0-7524-0309-5

LONDON
(Greater London and Middlesex)

Battersea and Clapham
Patrick Loobey
ISBN 0-7524-0010-X

Canning Town
Howard Bloch and Nick Harris
ISBN 0-7524-0057-6

Chiswick
Carolyn and Peter Hammond
ISBN 0-7524-0001-0

Forest Gate
Nick Harris and Dorcas Sanders
ISBN 0-7524-0049-5

Greenwich
Barbara Ludlow
ISBN 0-7524-0045-2

Highgate and Muswell Hill
Joan Schwitzer and Ken Gay
ISBN 0-7524-0119-X

Islington
Gavin Smith
ISBN 0-7524-0140-8

Lewisham
John Coulter and Barry Olley
ISBN 0-7524-0059-2

Leyton and Leytonstone
Keith Romig and Peter Lawrence
ISBN 0-7524-0158-0

Newham Dockland
Howard Bloch
ISBN 0-7524-0107-6

Norwood
Nicholas Reed
ISBN 0-7524-0147-5

Peckham and Nunhead
John D. Beasley
ISBN 0-7524-0122-X

Piccadilly Circus
David Oxford
ISBN 0-7524-0196-3

Stoke Newington
Gavin Smith
ISBN 0-7524-0159-9

Sydenham and Forest Hill
John Coulter and John Seaman
ISBN 0-7524-0036-3

Wandsworth
Patrick Loobey
ISBN 0-7524-0026-6

Wanstead and Woodford
Ian Dowling and Nick Harris
ISBN 0-7524-0113-0

MONMOUTHSHIRE

Vanished Abergavenny
Frank Olding
ISBN 0-7524-0034-7

Abertillery, Aberbeeg and Llanhilleth
Abertillery and District Museum Society and Simon Eckley
ISBN 0-7524-0134-3

Blaina, Nantyglo and Brynmawr
Trevor Rowson
ISBN 0-7524-0136-X

NORFOLK

North Norfolk
Cliff Richard Temple
ISBN 0-7524-0149-1

NOTTINGHAMSHIRE

Nottingham 1897–1947
Douglas Whitworth
ISBN 0-7524-0157-2

OXFORDSHIRE

Banbury
Tom Rigby
ISBN 0-7524-0013-4

PEMBROKESHIRE

Saundersfoot and Tenby
Ken Daniels
ISBN 0-7524-0192-0

RADNORSHIRE

Llandrindod Wells
Chris Wilson
ISBN 0-7524-0191-2

SHROPSHIRE

Leominster
Eric Turton
ISBN 0-7524-0307-9

Ludlow
David Lloyd
ISBN 0-7524-0155-6

Oswestry
Bernard Mitchell
ISBN 0-7524-0032-0

North Telford: Wellington, Oakengates, and Surrounding Areas
John Powell and Michael A. Vanns
ISBN 0-7524-0124-6

South Telford: Ironbridge Gorge, Madeley, and Dawley
John Powell and Michael A. Vanns
ISBN 0-7524-0125-4

SOMERSET

Bath
Paul De'Ath
ISBN 0-7524-0127-0

Around Yeovil
Robin Ansell and Marion Barnes
ISBN 0-7524-0178-5

STAFFORDSHIRE

Cannock Chase
Sherry Belcher and Mary Mills
ISBN 0-7524-0051-7

Around Cheadle
George Short
ISBN 0-7524-0022-3

The Potteries
Ian Lawley
ISBN 0-7524-0046-0

East Staffordshire
Geoffrey Sowerby and Richard Farman
ISBN 0-7524-0197-1

SUFFOLK

Lowestoft to Southwold
Humphrey Phelps
ISBN 0-7524-0108-4

Walberswick to Felixstowe
Humphrey Phelps
ISBN 0-7524-0109-2

SURREY

Around Camberley
Ken Clarke
ISBN 0-7524-0148-3

Around Cranleigh
Michael Miller
ISBN 0-7524-0143-2

Epsom and Ewell
Richard Essen
ISBN 0-7524-0111-4

Farnham by the Wey
Jean Parratt
ISBN 0-7524-0185-8

Industrious Surrey: Historic Images of the County at Work
Chris Shepheard
ISBN 0-7524-0009-6

Reigate and Redhill
Mary G. Goss
ISBN 0-7524-0179-3

Richmond and Kew
Richard Essen
ISBN 0-7524-0145-9

SUSSEX

Billingshurst
Wendy Lines
ISBN 0-7524-0301-X

WARWICKSHIRE

Central Birmingham 1870–1920
Keith Turner
ISBN 0-7524-0053-3

Old Harborne
Roy Clarke
ISBN 0-7524-0054-1

WILTSHIRE

Malmesbury
Dorothy Barnes
ISBN 0-7524-0177-7

Great Western Swindon
Tim Bryan
ISBN 0-7524-0153-X

Midland and South Western Junction Railway
Mike Barnsley and Brian Bridgeman
ISBN 0-7524-0016-9

WORCESTERSHIRE

Around Malvern
Keith Smith
ISBN 0-7524-0029-0

YORKSHIRE
(EAST RIDING)

Hornsea
G.L. Southwell
ISBN 0-7524-0120-3

YORKSHIRE
(NORTH RIDING)

Northallerton
Vera Chapman
ISBN 0-7524-055-X

Scarborough in the 1970s and 1980s
Richard Percy
ISBN 0-7524-0325-7

YORKSHIRE
(WEST RIDING)

Barnsley
Barnsley Archive Service
ISBN 0-7524-0188-2

Bingley
Bingley and District Local History Society
ISBN 0-7524-0311-7

Bradford
Gary Firth
ISBN 0-7524-0313-3

Castleford
Wakefield Metropolitan District Council
ISBN 0-7524-0047-9

Doncaster
Peter Tuffrey
ISBN 0-7524-0162-9

Harrogate
Malcolm Neesam
ISBN 0-7524-0154-8

Holme Valley
Peter and Iris Bullock
ISBN 0-7524-0139-4

Horsforth
Alan Cockroft and Matthew Young
ISBN 0-7524-0130-0

Knaresborough
Arnold Kellett
ISBN 0-7524-0131-9

Around Leeds
Matthew Young and Dorothy Payne
ISBN 0-7524-0168-8

Penistone
Matthew Young and David Hambleton
ISBN 0-7524-0138-6

Selby from the William Rawling Collection
Matthew Young
ISBN 0-7524-0198-X

Central Sheffield
Martin Olive
ISBN 0-7524-0011-8

Around Stocksbridge
Stocksbridge and District History Society
ISBN 0-7524-0165-3

TRANSPORT

Filton and the Flying Machine
Malcolm Hall
ISBN 0-7524-0171-8

Gloster Aircraft Company
Derek James
ISBN 0-7524-0038-X

Great Western Swindon
Tim Bryan
ISBN 0-7524-0153-X

Midland and South Western Junction Railway
Mike Barnsley and Brian Bridgeman
ISBN 0-7524-0016-9

Shorts Aircraft
Mike Hooks
ISBN 0-7524-0193-9

This stock list shows all titles available in the United Kingdom as at 30 September 1995.